A Meaningful Quest

A Meaningful Quest

Marta Atougato

RESOURCE *Publications* · Eugene, Oregon

A MEANINGFUL QUEST

Resource Publications
An Imprint of Wipf and Stock Publishers
199 W. 8th Ave., Suite 3
Eugene, OR 97401

www.wipfandstock.com

PAPERBACK ISBN: 979-8-3852-1495-2
HARDCOVER ISBN: 979-8-3852-1496-9
EBOOK ISBN: 979-8-3852-1497-6

VERSION NUMBER 05/22/24

For those who find in poetry their
very own search engine.

Contents

Acknowledgments

First of all I would like to convey an immense sense of gratitude for all the beauty that surrounds me and the ability to recognize it.

I would like to thank my mother for her clarity of mind and unlimited faith.

To my best friend, twin soul and also cousin Virginia, who always listens, and her unwavering belief in me. Her strength is nothing but inspiring. She is just incredible!

To my daughter Carolina, for rocking my world every single day. Without the three of you, I don't think I would've tried harder.

To my other best friend Cristina and her lovely daughters, Constança and Vitória, for her continuous support, kindness and guidance.

To my special nephews Guilherme and David, for always laughing with me. Together, we have huge amounts of fun. Let's keep it up, boys!

To dad and brother Kico for caring.

Also, huge thanks to cousins Sílvia and Catarina, whose joy and availability to help are invaluable to me, as well as all other close family members for their encouragement.

Thank you, Jorge, for doing the research.

Thank you, Helena and Fátima, for your kind friendship.

Thank you, Paulo, for being there.

Thank you to all my adult learners for sharing so much with me.

Thank you, reader, for taking the time to read my poems.

Non Days

As days go by
And months move on,
Ahead of my lifeline,
I feel very little.
All sorts of things seem brittle
And tangible at the same time.

My hand hoovers like
A protest lurking
With its meaningful nothing,
To be heard later,
When the archives fall silent
And ruthlessness takes over,
Medieval, in its core.

Loud and bright days and
Nights and blissful mornings and
Matching evenings and
All that warmth is
Mere absence.

Deliberate, the scream before
The voice, reveals,
Out loud, the content of
Ancient riots
Turned new hereafter,
In perpetuity.

Damage,
No longer contained, is
Self-imposed, within
The exhaustion existing in
The non days of our lives.

Colliding Self

Too many colliding intentions
From those who want to help
But can't, are settled in
My mind for proper selection.

My weariness relies upon their
Kindness for the betterment of
All breaches, remaining in the
Pavement I tread on, but little
Gets sorted out.

It's sometimes too abrupt to
Acknowledge a coexisting reality
Of sticky counterfeit emotions
I seek to let loose, but won't.

I dwell on a myriad of
Entangled expectations and
Conjured temptations.

Procrastinating my own
Existence, embracing other
People's coexistence as far
As my distorted bemusement
Goes free, I choose to breathe.

The Silhouette

There's a Silhouette resting
On that man's shoulder
With her own agenda
In mind.

Bothered by his peaceful demeanor,
Marveled by his resolute brushstrokes,
She aims at quenching her thirst
Through the man's endeavor.

He stands alone and forlorn each
Time he takes the nurses' pills.
As he withers, his work becomes a
Solemn constellation encased
In a parched canvas.

Knowing it will all be forgotten as
Quickly as the brushstrokes of
The demented painter, the
Silhouette plans to mingle with
The established scenery.

Lazy Day

On a glorious day
I linger.
I linger as if laziness
Is my motto,
Appraised goal, highly
Recommended for fallen
Victims of burnout
Syndrome in denial.

Stretching out as the gorgeous
Felines most times do,
I muse over the
Reason Sapiens left
The caves in the first place . . .
Such cozy hideout
From a lifetime of
Scientific implementation,
Statistical quantification and
Consecutive labor days.

Masons, we became, scaffolding
Intensely for a higher purpose;
Shepherds turned into
Avid potato traders and
Wine makers.

Still, I linger
Over a glass of
Portuguese Port Wine
From the Douro Vineyards.

As of now,
I am withdrawn.
Quarrels and banters are
No longer to be heard
Or noticed.
I am caved in by
My own choosing.
In my secluded oyster
I will, for all times,
Remain:

Unattached
Unavailable
Uninterested

Overplanning

When waking up to a false start,
The day begins still.
Nothing becomes bearable or
Preferable, all options hostile,
All fragments loose.
Living, itself, hides
An indelible goal:
Crave nothing.

Brave acceptance,
When expectation is expected.
A misconception of sorts,
Wrong and empty
Before a clear path
Is unveiled,
Not drawn at all,
Just experienced,
And valid
And truthful
And vivid
And meaningful.

So pure,
The swirl
Of emotions
Finally
Resets.

Abandonment

If dark is the staining color
And absence of light
A soulful shade,
I shall whisper words
No more and lay
Where silence
Uncovers mightiness
Within my grasp.

If never again
In sight of brittle
Virtue or disdain
I weaken thoughts
Of never-ending hopefulness,
I shall quit
And leave in foreseeable
Abandonment.

If solace complies
Once more with
The damaged decay
Left untouched,
I shall go,
Moving endlessly
Towards the mountain and
In confinement,
Offer my rendition
To the passers-by
As punishment, for my deserved penalty.

Scarcity

There's not much left in times like these.
Scarcity preys at will
Malevolent, belligerent . . .
Only Oddity remains,
Mocking the obsolete resilience
Still afloat,

Over the decomposing nothingness
Burdened by guilt;

Over the decomposing ailments,
Numb, pitiful;

Over the decomposing vacant prayers
Deemed redeeming yet redundant.

Does the soul comply with programming?
Does love crave blissful awakenings?
Does a broken heart mend sorrowfully?
Does power stay after loss?

Your eyes are hungry.
Mine? Just anemic.

Scarcity has left abruptly
Living now by the water,
Feeding off the fate of others.

Consumers Daily

Today I went out.
I went out to go shopping.
I went shopping for items.
For items
I cannot live without.
Items I cannot bear the absence of.
Items I really need.
Items I must have.
Items invaluable to me.
Just items, really.

I bought coffee and dark chocolate,
Apples and watermelon,
Pasta and mushrooms.

I bought shampoo and hairspray,
A moisturizer and a body scrub,
Tampons and cotton disks,
Bottles of water and bottles of wine.
A box of condoms too.

I bought a poetry book, of course,
And a smaller one with relaxing mandalas
To paint.

I bought another dress and
Another bracelet,
A pair of ethnic earrings
Suitable for pierced ears
Like mine.

I bought shinny hairpins and happiness.
I bought tastiness and flavor.
I bought comfort and commodity.
I bought easiness and trust.
I bought frivolity and vainness.
I bought lust and pleasure.

I bought a lot.
I got very little.

End of the Day

After a day's work,
After the job's done,
Resetting seems proper:
We reunite over dinner
In dire search for
Something else.

We feed.
We talk trifles.
We savor dessert.
We sit and listen.
We brush our teeth.
We're in the bedroom.
We undress.
We lay in bed.
We touch.
We are love.
We are content.

The day has already
Wrapped itself long ago
And we wonder
Why it always ends
So elusive,
So vacant,
So polluted.

The Song

The sad, sad song playing from the neighbors attic
Hurts, like the scent of rain
Touching dehydrated soil for the first time
After summer.

Magnificent, tells tails of those
Who didn't make it, while crossing
Native lands and mighty seas,
Banned from memory failure.

Encouraging, keeps going,
The chorus sings perseverance;
Tenacity fed them well
Pushing back floods and droughts.

Immense, in its own harmony,
Delays a well-established outcome;
Depicts the damaged algorithm
Carved in numbers
Never understood,
Always misinterpreted,
Like that righteous road map
We once tried
And then neglected.

No Good at All

I'm the pissed off irritating angel
The Gods have purged from above.

Angels are just metaphors
Conjured to wreck our sense of purity.

No one in despair leaves an angel untouched.
Broken wings, majestic sorrow,
But nothing can be done.

Wings darkened by sudden wrath,
Blood taints their vows.

Angels fly within the mind,
Carve new thoughts in spirits high above.

Is redemption attainable?
Is decay avoidable?
Cause we're up to no good . . .

Boredom

Bored out of her mind,
She just wanted to pick her nose.

Something quite disgusting but
She took great pleasure in doing,
However far from being politically or
Socially correct in the context
She was in.

The options were limited.

She could either get out,
Walk away from there, the epicenter of her boredom,
Or simply stay and give it a try.

Huge effort required to implement
The second possibility.

At least she wasn't thinking about
Picking her nose anymore.

She wanted to engage in other activities,
Free herself from the shackles of duty,
Responsibility, expectation, and have
Her own moment of enjoyment and pleasure . . .

She took a deep breath and carried on.

She didn't want to be there at all
But, at the same time,
She felt she just had to stay.

So, she stayed, more focused, more
Willing, more interested,
But still quite bored.

Evasion

When I travel
I breathe more:
Lungs widen desperate
For foreign CO_2.

But the *tempo*
Is wrong and cut off:
Cannot breathe deeply,
Cannot live immensely . . .

Is chaos troublesome?
It reveals cravings
I do not wish to acknowledge.
I find them shallow.
Perhaps too blurry,
Perhaps too unruly,
Perhaps too exuberant
For such brittle
Understanding of all things
Unstable, echoing quietly
Beneath the Dura
Perilously settling in . . .

Traveling won't take me that far;
New sightings are taking over.

Suddenly, the backyard
Of certain thoughts
Seems wide enough.

Transitioning

When she walks upon land,
When she climbs a ladder,
Elements are lost and
Faith withers.

Rain falls,
Silently soft and subtle
Barely making itself
Known or felt.

Wisdom settles in.
She needs to listen,
She needs to understand!
But no one calls out the name
She so avidly embraced in the past
Only to remove from the future.

She's free now.
Her scent is quiet,
Her body dormant
Yet fertile.

She will return one day
As the Goddess who
Lost her bearings and
Became something else.

Whispers

Abruptly, the song ended.
Few noticed.
Silence overcame
The noise
As it always does.
There was a sharp edge to
The promise left by
That pungent song
No one cared for.

Some voices
Kept whispering
Yet singing
In disguise of a
Heart felt compulsion.

There's innuendo and blame.
This song should be quieted.

Beyond all constraints, someone
Scattered the words...
Brave offering to the wind!

Verbs were picked up
Here and there;
Nouns lit up by translucent
Voices echoing inside
The lighthouse,
Battered by the tides,
Protected by the sea.

Revolt

There is a mutiny in sight.
On the road,
Statistically different people
Protest. They say
Their hunger is ancient,
Their pain forgotten
Over and over.
First, they asked.
After, they put it on paper.
Now, a riot is in progress:
Throats scream sarcasm,
Tongues spit
Words of fiery
Unsolicited facts,
Closed fists demand
What others are not prepared
To acknowledge.
Righteousness stands akin to understanding . . .

My knees
Bend in dismay.
Worn out like a kitchen cloth,
I have nothing
To protest about.

Scented Skin

Your scent,
When we wake up embracing as we were one,
Is like the cinnamon I
Require in my espresso coffee:
Intense, sensual, a little
Bitter but, straight off,
All inner warmth reveled.

I take it plain,
No sugar in it, for
Sweetness easily falls
Prey to a crowd of wanted
Hidden flavors.

I acknowledge your crude
Self. I welcome the conflicted
Reasoning your nakedness fails
To comply with.

Once awake, your delirious
Status subsides, connecting to a
Plausible reality
Already taking place
Within your ethos.

Too hectic a burden you
Carry, insanely aware of
All things unfazed.

For now, weariness has
Left the room. Only the
Creases in your cinnamon
Scented skin remain the same,
As the awarded token
Still in debt,
Still in silence,
Beneath your breading.

The Aftermath

The Aftermath
Screams insanity, rage,
And hides no longer.
On the streets,
Troubles move deeply
Tattooed in frail bodies.
There's nowhere to run
And there's everywhere to run to . . .
Nonetheless,
No serenity will be found.
The sun is there, still,
Devoid of warmth.
The sea waves crash ashore,
Just moving really,
For no strength lies underneath the tides.

Somewhere in the yard
The strawberries dried out long ago, but
The turnips survived, though.
There will be soup for dinner!
Now it's pouring down hard once more
But maybe this time,
Just this one time,
A good meal survives
The Aftermath of our times.

Ode to Reading

Open a book more often.

Read, out loud, to yourself
If for no one else, or
To a lost crowd
Of random listeners
Willing to pause on the
Sidewalk, before duty
Becomes reason enough
To comply with it.

Open a book more often.

Connect to the gleaming
Pages of entangled words on
A level only known to
Yourself and allow
Them to engage: be
Heard, be felt, be wanted.
Keep the secret when understanding;
Tell the story while interpreting.

Open a book more often.

Redirect all other
Pungent realities at
Hand to another day.
Focus on yourself and the
Book. Build a relationship:
Books have feelings too.
Don't crease the pages!
Don't stain the content!

Open a book more often.

A paper back edition,
For sure.

Another Side of Contemporary Living

The shops were crowded.
Happy people in a frenzy.
Carefully selected items being tried and bought.
Careless bags being carried around.
Ecstatic people purchasing their way out of nothing at all.

Still,
No malice, no agenda . . .

Just a warm embrace
From the posh side of life.

To the Park

Early morning,
When I go to the park,
The light strikes differently
And so does living.

The old couple dressed in purple?
They must love each other very much,
Because their running is like
A trustworthy syncopated marathon.

The lady feeding the children?
She must love all of them very much,
Because she baked them a heart-shaped
Red velvet cake with cream.

The young man and the blind girl?
He must love this girl very much,
Because he blocked his eyesight and
Stretched out his hands to meet hers.

The crazy dog with a limp?
He must love that man very much,
Because he brings him perfectly shaped
Sticks and stones from across the park.

Me? Well, I must love this park very much,
Because I realized that life's itineraries
Come and go in the solemn details
Of this park.

Sea Level

When the Sea has nightmares,
The waves become its fearful wrath,
Which doesn't subside easily, because
The Sea is grand.

In awe, people say
"The Sea is beautiful today"
Reflecting upon the troubled swirl
And their constrained self-awareness.

Memories trump the waves;
Memories embody the Sea level
Raising, right outside our doorstep,
Drowning all the food lovingly
Planted in the backyard of
The unquenchable garden, one
Day, most hope to plough
Quietly.

Thoughts and Queries

Almost fallen,
Contemporary legends still
Fill in a vacant space.
Their echoes are like
Incantations, their content
Like a revelation: resilient,
Resourceful, ours to
Defend and perpetuate.
Tightly bound,
Neatly gathered.

Adrenaline seems not
Enough to fight off
The fear. Myriads adrift
Are convening, anxious to
Finally exude all fears.

Trapped in a kaleidoscope,
Some queries are finally
Coming through.
A shared commitment:
Reveal all sorts of
Exotic intentions relevant
For a vehement debate.

I want to foster new theories;
I need to participate in depth.

Being curious for long
Enough, has also
Made me aware.

Outside the Office

Outside,
Opposite from where I
Sit, there's plenty.

Towards the end of the
Day, all elements
Become pristine.
Something remarkable, to
Be noticed about the
Mid-afternoon light
Regardless the weather.

I'm encased in its
Warmth and I feel
Just fine.
Outside, an encrypted
Message available for
Decoding, lures me in.

I rush past my boss,
My co-workers and
Other staff as well.
I rush to be out in
The open and breathe
Effortlessly, stripped of
Issues of the laypeople
And ascend.

Once roaming outside, I
Also nurture quietly.
All steps joyful, leading
Nowhere in particular
Aimlessly recovering from
Too much, too hasty,
Too quickly, too scared . . .

Limited as is, my
Peripheral understanding is
Savvy too: I'm urged
On a quest to fight
Away empty shells and
Dull hysteria.

To the Shore

I gather the vigorous
Forces within the inner voices.
Ancient glories amidst
Our fortune.

Ahead of time,
Stranded in a secluded
Beach somewhere on the
Coastline, the Prophet's trophies
Were left there,
Inadvertently, crushed by a
Hasty decision.

Trophies they are,
Nonetheless, still abiding
Coexisting patterns,
Often disregarded, like the
Mighty wingspan
Of a bird.

I carve all dismay in
Cobblestones; I rush my
Awkwardly irregular
Handwriting towards
Better words and
Wiser rhymes.

The flow is never-ending.
The change is ever-increasing.
As infinity settles, next to my
Proverbial nothingness.

Footprint on Your Moon

If the crashing site
Grows flowers, you already
Know what it means:
Closure was brought upon
A much needed ending.
You can breathe again.
You can portray your existence
In a wider frame.
Let the little flowers grow.
Let them scatter their
Glittering warmth
Around. Embrace their
Colored magical ways.
The *tempo* is indelible.
There isn't enough land
To run in despair
And still escape;
Nor enough reason to
Wander aimlessly and
Still loose yourself timelessly.
Credit yourself a
Worthy footprint.

Your presence is the iridescent
Moon in the overwhelming sky.

Don't let the
Myths tell you
Otherwise.

Felines They Are

My ginger cat is
At odds with my
Calico cat.
They both want
The same cozy
Spot, which is
My lap.

Hush boys, hush!
My fondness for you
Will never be limited
By my physical self!

Poetry 24/7

I'm so glad
There is poetry,
I must say!

Its existence
Makes you and me
Stronger and wiser;
It allows a better understanding
Of both the simple and the complex.

Our humanity expanded
Beyond imposed borders
Of self-doubt and self-restraint.

I wonder in whose mind the
First verse was chiseled,
And later blown into
The passing wind.

Perhaps it was simply
Uttered, in the hope of
Being heard, not seen
Or found at all.

Perhaps it was merely a
Heart-felt compulsion, coaxed
Out of an enduring love,
And cheer perseverance.

As it is today.

A Long Time Ago

Once I walked towards
The circle. The inner
Circle, the outer life,
The vivid insight,
The heart-felt intensity,
The raging conflict,
The imminent resolution,
The mature outcome.

Once I envisioned
A light. A bright light,
A fresh beginning,
A daunting new,
A fierce compulsion,
A powerful leap,
A steady road map,
A never-ending quest.

Once I clung on reveries.
Alluring reveries,
Shared pleasures,
Igniting thoughts,
A mighty presence,
Unsolvable riddle,
Unforeseeable translation,
A prosperous emancipation.

But right now, something
Has changed abruptly:
I've decided to
Live and breathe in a parallel
Reality, without redemption.

Shaping

The strongest bond has been
Perpetuated. The lovely people
And the lovely days are
Prosperous and fertile.
Blissful singularities,
Down the road from
Where I chose to live.

I find myself thrown
Against rough walls of
Reasoning. Still captive, my
Brittle senses are born and
Nurtured in the realm of
Their own secrecy,
Oblivious and carefree.

I greet the wonders
Of the past only to
Regain the consciousness,
Now restored, in
My imminent faith.

Capsizing

Your pheromones are weary and
You smell of distrust.

I can't appease your
Headache nor the slopes
Of desire you've failed to
Climb; the accomplishment of nothing
That leaves you right where you
Started: inwardly at a loss,
While eating a mountain of
Blueberries and strawberries
Too bitter for your
Own understanding.
Then, you mourn
While laughing;
Then, you get back up
Again, while grieving.
Have you brushed all
Your teeth yet?
Have you counted all
The clouds above your
Self-centered ceiling?

Don't be lead by
Fortune or obtuse faith;
Don't be tainted by
Bad omens and
Credible misconceptions.

You must
Sort it
All out
By yourself.

The Search

The narrow streets cramping
My hasty steps, on the left
Of the sidewalk,
Are nearly over.
My yearning is now within the
Boundaries of the acceptable behavior
We have all come to
Foster lovingly.

Still, I'm eager to set a
Path and stride, lightheartedly,
On any road. Shall I carry a
Map? Shall see a fortune teller?
My faith is tainted and blurred by
The unforeseen wrath
Of a mystic crowd.

Vaguely, I recognize consistencies
And many hopeful words,
To distinguish and decipher.

I'm set on a quest to
Strengthen a forlorn desire,
Brought back, by a set of
Meaningful life-altering events.

In Doubt

Do you wish to
Acknowledge a truth?

A truth is rare and
Bothers, most of the time.
It is known for its
Contempt and lacks
Empathy. It is what
It is, and one must
Decide: am I stable
Enough to observe
Beyond my quest?
Refrain from the need
To interfere, accept
The stains, make a
Bonfire, and meditate
By the flames?

Is a truth the truth?
Perhaps not. I fail
To understand the man
Who once fostered a
Rotten ideal, too beautiful
To be destroyed, on
His own accord.

Is the sun a contemporary
Finite source? Perhaps not.
Warmth doesn't always
Come from the outside.
One should pick sudden
Sparks, here and there,
And, if derailing, go
Back, pick some more.

There is no latent tragedy
In sight; no catharsis is
Taking place in the
Universe, as we sparkle.
Only a truth lies among
The common speech.
Benevolently, it is soothing
Any mistrust placed in
The common ground,
Beneath the feet,
Out of cheer guilt.

Framed

Oil on canvas: I am a painting!
Standing by myself in
This immense gallery, I am
Beautiful, nonetheless.
All others have been purchased,
Admired, scrutinized,
And later, forgotten.

Unescorted, I still hold the vivid
Colors and the frame
That keep me going.

Alive

Elusive bonds enclosed
By grief, in a finite
Existence, are yet worth another
Minute. Revisiting layers of the
Self, tightly bound to a unique
Dominion, joyous, uncompromising,
Where havoc stands absent,
I gradually unfold from
The cause of it all.

Observing from a distance,
Every course of action seems
Tenacious enough to follow
And engage. I want to go
Further and trod on the
Inequalities that rendered me
Unfit for the duty of loving.

Outside the chrysalis,
Competition proves easier and
Fulfillment attainable.

Step forth, build momentum,
Stay alert, because

There is a sequence of
Grace to be respected

And a pattern of
Gratitude to be voiced.

Moving on

The armored sentiment,
Once described as
Perilous, transitioned.

The process entailed
Abundant uneasiness, restlessness,
And self-doubt.

It carved on the skin the
Odor of time elapsing
Quickly. It felt both
Wrong and right and
All sureness around the sun
Spelt sacrifice, because
Unquenchable thoughts
Have just collapsed,
As mere myths.

Guilt

The dark circles you carry
Under the eyes, are the center
Of the Universe coming to
Terms with itself through yourself.

Caught in the echoing swirl
Of a song that leaps into
Your mind, into the servitude
Of time, as a piece of
News collapsing on
Your doorstep,
No wire will bind
Your will again!

Sleepless nights may
Happen, notwithstanding, but
Notice the unprecedented
Inquires of your mind's
Resolve, free from conflicting
Exhortations and mainstream guilt.

When singing is dire,
Play the music and
Elaborate on the chords
That will eventually
Damage your fingers.

Then, add a voice and
Improvise, because the dark
Circles you carry under
The eyes, are anathema to
Your Universe, unfolding.

Purge

Inadvertently, I picked an
Apple from the fruit basket
And washed it thoroughly,
Disabling the most resilient
Bacteria, perilously lurking in
Its golden shaped glory.

It was the transparency of
The water that caught my
Eye, though.

So, in the absence of
Listeners, I though
To myself: how pure
Water is!
How pristine!
How immaculate!
How benevolent its
Intent: to quench one's
Thirst and cleanse
One's colon!

Loss

When thunder points to the mountain,
Unleashes power, unleashes mightiness.

I feel the claustrophobic despair
Of being hunted
By nothing at all.

I want depth I can see
In the eyes of others,
Reflected in mirrors, like bonfires.

In the flesh, the whip is long gone
But they still want to pluck out the pale dignity
Somewhere, left behind.

Drained.
Disoriented.
Loss of faith,
If it ever existed at all . . .

Error; Begin Again

It started out as a bit of a fluke;
A stroke of serendipity!

It was really just a blunder, a silly
Inaccuracy, an emotional slip,
A syntax misrepresentation of
One's thoughts.

Then, it escalated, becoming a sudden
Change of perspective, a change
Of heart, a change of mindset.

Now, I dare ask: are you troubled
By your own guilt? The guilt
That makes one crouch and slouch
And shiver as if the weight of the
Biggest mammal on Earth watches
You sleep at night?

Let it go, I say!
Let it consume itself in its own grandeur!
Let it become the supreme trait that
Monitors your oddity and
Turns you into another flawed
Human, on his way
To make it right
This time.

Ability

Can you hear them?
Can you really?

Can you hear the wind, the sea,
The chirping, the howling,
The cracking, the laughter,
The crying, the whispering,
And the singing?

Can you do it?
Can you really?

Can you clap your hands and
Snap your fingers to the rhythm of
A tune, greet your elders and
Your friends and be sure to
Say "see you tomorrow", buy
A book or a ticket to
Some artist's venue, do your
Laundry on any week day,
And book a short
Bed and breakfast holiday?

Can you feel?
Can you really?

Can you pet your cat but let
Your hand upon its coat spell
Freedom and respect? Can
You walk in the park and stop
To admire the twisted trees?
Are you afraid of spiders and
Snakes but feel brave enough to
Acknowledge their existence and carry on?

With love,
The writer of this poem

The Brain and the Bean

Apart from what I've experienced,
I know very little, probably nothing at all.

My brain knows Maths, but Maths doesn't count;
My brain knows History, but History doesn't count;
My brain knows French, but French doesn't count;
Physics and Spanish don't count either . . .

Too much time and effort is
Put into shaping one's head
And silencing one's heart.

Hence, a story: "The Brain and the Bean",
The last one throbbing
Inside one's rib cage,
Encapsulated, unfit for the
Squared existence we strive for.

Sapienazing the Sapiens has
Left a profound footprint
Not only on the Moon . . .

Perils come and go; however, they
Will never really leave, and
The purest feelings become
Counterfeit prerogatives for the
Twenty-first century.

I once opened a book for
The Brain to chew on, while
The Bean was momentarily set
On a quest of its own.
I no longer keep birds in cages, you know . . .

The Look

There's a gaze upon us.
It's their gaze that moves on us,
A gaze that pries shall
Never encounter our eyes.
My plight,
Because you are my
Personal demon
In sight.

Floating

The pending leaf
Hanging from above is,
In itself, the worldly metaphor
Of hopeful solace
Today seems to bring.

She stands by herself,
The only leaf in that twisted
Tree; its only spark
Of joyful beauty.

It stands alone against
The vicious wind
And fierce rain.

The elements are hard
To bear with.
The mighty leaf
Conveys her best

As most surely try to.

Flourishing

In exchange for a wild blossom,
Bring a joyous sentiment!
A fierce emotion, that won't
Collapse under certain bittersweet
Life-changing events, appearing
Unannounced, in the vicinity
Of one's cozy existence.

Constrained by my being
Human, I quiver at the thought
Of losing perspective and
Face deception, when
Deception isn't necessarily
My foe. Still, a condescending
Demeanor occurs.

Be mindful of the existing wild
Blossoms out there to be
Exchanged for a portfolio of
Sagacious resolutions and
Avid commitments.

Wild blossoms belong to the realm
Of unyielding new beginnings;
Wild blossoms carry the weight
Of the mighty treasure;
Wild blossoms are so
Underrated these days . . .

Just Rain

On a greyish rainy day
There's much stepping on
Sidewalks, while eluding
Puddles, as if people
Fear the given water.

Do people fear the rain?
People probably fear the rain,
Because winter clothes
Are harder to wear
And more difficult
To dry out.

Confiscated

I neglected my eagerness,
The core of all interests
And intentions too.

The signs were sworn,
Reflecting shameless need
And greedy sorrow.

Keeping afloat, for a
Penny worth of hungry
Senses and wild anger,
I starved for knowledge.

Deprived of real wisdom,
I tempered with the
Intermittent fasting imposed
Upon myself,
On track, to purify
Mischievous moments.

Granddad's Been in the War

I.
The abyss was in plain sight.

In the line of fire
Soldiers wept: tormented
Men with bruised
Bodies and dormant
Souls, too anguished to
Be awoken.

Pain and immense suffering
Are never absent in a war.

Where is the enemy?
Are they my enemy?

II.
He scarcely said anything.
Just one or two light episodes of war
Suitable for all ears . . .

He did comment on the
Permanent hunger though . . .

He did comment on the
Snowy days on end, numbing the limbs . . .

He did write a diary
Accounting for all seen and felt war atrocities
He couldn't verbalize . . .

III.
My Granddad was a tall sturdy man
Who endured the war,
Returned home,
Lead a quiet life,
And once saved me
From a rabid
Colony of ants,
I was, inadvertently, standing on
At the age of three.

This poem is dedicated to my Grandfather who bravely fought
in World War I, whom I barely knew.

Perfumed

The other day was
A scented day.

Involuntarily, people dreamt more
Than usual. Many rituals
Were enriched by honest
Sharing and devotion.

Dancing aimlessly was a valid
Action, taking many majestic
Shapes and forms
Long forlorn.

An immense song filled
The atmosphere, backed by
The pungent chords of one
Thousand random guitars
Of all colors,

And the music was the best
Omen, while waiting for other
Magnificent scented days
Yet to come.

Every Breath

The Sun rises everyday
For everybody.

Sometimes you can see it,
Sometimes you cannot.

But breathing is an
Endeavor to be accomplished
On your own, out of the limelight.